Can
Science
Solve?

# The Mystery of Atlantis

**Holly Wallace**

Heinemann Library
Chicago, Illinois

© 1999 Reed Educational and Professional Publishing
Published by Heinemann Library,
an imprint of Reed Educational & Professional Publishing,
Chicago, IL

Customer Service 888-454-2279
Visit our website at www.heinemannlibrary.com

Designed by AMR

Cover photograph reproduced with permission of Ronald Sheridan, Ancient Art and Architecture Collection.

Printed in Hong Kong

03
10 9 8 7 6 5 4

**Library of Congress Cataloging-in-Publication Data**
Wallace, Holly, 1961-
    The mystery of Atlantis / Holly Wallace.
        p. cm.— (Can science solve?)
    Includes bibliographical references.
    Summary: Examines the legend of the lost civilization of Atlantis and various theories that seek to explain it.
    ISBN 1-57572-803-6 (lib. bdg.)
    1. Atlantis—Juvenile literature. [1. Atlantis.]   I. Title.
II. Series.
GN751.W35 1999
001.94—dc21                                    98-54490
                                                    CIP
                                                    AC

**Acknowledgments**

The Publishers would like to thank the following for permission to reproduce photographs:

Ancient Art and Architecture Collection, p.11; R. Sheridan, pp. 8, 18, 19; G. Tortoli, pp.16, 20; Fortean Picture Library, pp. 7, 10; K. Aarsleff, p. 13; J. and C. Bord, p. 22; W. Donato, pp. 25, 27; Llewellyn Publications, p. 24; Ronald Grant Collection, p. 5; Oxford Scientific Films/R. Packwood, p.14; Science Photo Library, p. 6; D. Parker, p. 12; Still Pictures/C. Guarita, p. 28.

Every effort has been made to contact copyright holders of any material reproduced in this book. Any omissions will be rectified in subsequent printings if notice is given to the publisher.

Some words are shown in bold, **like this**. You can find out what they mean by looking in the glossary.

# Contents

Unsolved Mysteries ................................4

Beginnings of a Mystery .......................6

What Was Atlantis Like?......................8

Interest Renewed ................................10

Other Theories....................................12

Atlantis Found? ..................................14

Earth Movements................................16

Looking at the Past .............................18

A Violent Volcano ..............................20

Other Sunken Cities ...........................22

Strange Stories ...................................24

A False Start.......................................26

In Conclusion ....................................28

*Glossary*...............................................*30*

*More Books to Read*............................*31*

*Index* ...................................................*32*

# Unsolved Mysteries

For centuries, people have been puzzled and fascinated by mysterious creatures, events, and places. Is there really a monster living in Loch Ness? Are UFOs tricks of the light or vehicles from outer space? Who is responsible for mysterious crop circle patterns—clever hoaxers or alien beings? Did the lost land of Atlantis ever exist? Some of these mysteries even puzzle scientists. Many scientists have spent years trying to find answers. But just how far can science go? Can it really explain the seemingly unexplainable? Are there some mysteries that science simply cannot solve? Read on, and make up your own mind.

This book tells you about the **legendary** lost land of Atlantis. It presents the only account that exists of the city, written by Plato in the 4th century B.C. It details later theories about the geographical, **archaeological**, and historical theories about its existence and destruction.

## What was Atlantis?

According to legend, Atlantis was an ancient island **civilization** in the Atlantic Ocean that flourished about 12,000 years ago. Then, in one night and a day, it sank without trace. Atlantis was a powerful kingdom. Its army had conquered large parts of Africa and Europe before being defeated by the Ancient Greeks. Its people enjoyed a **privileged** lifestyle. They surrounded themselves with fine things and beautiful palaces. Then, one fateful day, their golden world came crashing down around them.

But did Atlantis ever exist? We have no eyewitness reports to go by. No ruins have ever been found. Only one ancient account exists. Later accounts have often been based more in science fiction than in science fact. If Atlantis did exist, two burning questions still remain—where was it located and where did it go? Was it destroyed by a natural disaster or an act of the gods? Is there anything science can do to solve one of the greatest mysteries of all?

Many books and films have been based on the story of Atlantis, including this one, entitled The Lost Kingdom. *This is a scene inside the fabulous royal palace of the Atlantean king.*

# Beginnings of a Mystery

The earliest and only written sources we have for the mystery of Atlantis are two ancient accounts. The Greek **philosopher** Plato wrote them in the 4th century B.C. They are written as dialogues, or conversations. The dialogues are between the philosopher Socrates and three friends. The two accounts are called *Timaeus* and *Critias*, the names of the main characters. Plato began to work on a third account but he never completed it.

Plato, the Greek philosopher, lived from 428–347 B.C. The legend of Atlantis was publicized through his writings. No one knows for sure if his works are fact or fiction.

## Two accounts

In his version of events, Plato tells the story of Atlantis through the poet and historian Critias. He says that he heard the story as a child from his grandfather, who had heard it from his own father. He, in turn, had heard it from his friend Solon (640?–558? B.C), a famous Greek politician from Athens. Solon had been told the story by an elderly Egyptian priest. The priest got the story from ancient temple records. The story begins about 9,000 years before Solon's birth—about 12,000 years ago. The story describes Atlantis as a rich, powerful island in the Atlantic Ocean. It says that its armies conquered many of the lands around the Mediterranean. They were finally defeated by the Athenians. This is Plato's account of the Egyptian priest's story:

"There was an island situated in front of the **straits** which you call the Pillars of Hercules, now called the Straits of Gibraltar, and which was larger than Libya and Asia Minor—now called Turkey—put together.... Now on this island of Atlantis there was a great and wonderful **empire** which ruled over the whole island and several others, and over parts of the **continent**, and controlled, within the straits, Libya as far as Egypt and Europe as far as Tyrrhenia, or Italy. This vast power attempted to **subdue** both my country, Egypt, and yours, Greece, and the whole region within the strait. Then, Solon, your country defeated the invaders and saved us all from slavery. But afterwards, there occurred violent earthquakes and floods, and in a single day and night, the island of Atlantis was swallowed up by the sea and disappeared..."

*A map of Atlantis from the 1644 book* Mundus Subterraneus *[The Underground World], by Dutch writer Athanasius Kircher. He used Plato's accounts to make this map.*

7

# What Was Atlantis Like?

In his second account, *Critias*, Plato described the history, geography, and people of Atlantis in more detail. He tells how the kings of Atlantis were created by Poseidon, the Ancient Greek god of the sea. Atlanteans were great architects and engineers. They built temples, palaces, and harbors. They built their capital city on a hill. It was circular in shape and surrounded by alternating rings of land and water. These rings were connected by bridges and tunnels. A huge canal joined the outermost ring of water to the sea. Behind the city was a great, fertile plain where farmers grew the city's food. The island was also rich in minerals, timber, and exotic animals, including elephants.

*According to legend, the people of Atlantis were descended from the god of the sea, Poseidon. Atlantis is named after Atlas, another Greek god.*

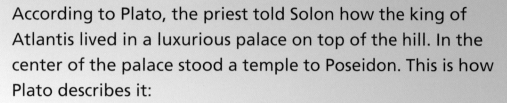

An artist's idea of what the gardens of the magnificent palace of the king of Atlantis looked like.

## A magnificent palace

According to Plato, the priest told Solon how the king of Atlantis lived in a luxurious palace on top of the hill. In the center of the palace stood a temple to Poseidon. This is how Plato describes it:

> "The outside of the temple was covered in silver, apart from the **pinnacles**. The pinnacles were covered in gold. Inside, the roof was made of ivory, decorated with gold, silver, and other precious metals. All the other walls and pillars were lined with precious metals. In the temple, they placed golden statues—there was Poseidon himself standing in a chariot pulled by six winged horses, and of such a size that he touched the roof of the temple with his head...."

It seemed the Atlanteans had everything they could wish for. But, says Plato, they became greedy and corrupt. Zeus, the king of the gods, decided to teach them a lesson. He destroyed their golden land as punishment.

Fifty years after his death, doubts arose as to whether Plato's Atlantis was a real place. People questioned the source of the story. Had it truly been passed down from one generation to the next? Or had Plato made it up? Was he really describing his own city, Athens? Was the account historical fact or fiction? The debate continues today.

# Interest Renewed

Modern interest in Atlantis began in the 19th century. An book called *Atlantis, the Antediluvian World* was published in 1882. An American politician, Ignatius Donnelly, wrote the story. The book quickly became a world-wide best-seller. The **cult** of Atlantis was born.

## Donnelly's theory

Donnelly honestly believed that Atlantis existed and was lost as Plato described. He placed the island in the Azores, in the mid-Atlantic Ocean. He argued his point with "several distinct and novel propositions."

*This is the cover of Donnelly's best-selling book* Atlantis, the Antediluvian World. *It sparked interest in the mystery of Atlantis.*

This is what he claimed:
- A large island, Atlantis, once existed in the Atlantic Ocean. It was all that remained of an Atlantic continent.
- Plato's description was historical fact.
- **Civilization** itself began in Atlantis.
- Atlantis was a mighty power that conquered many other countries.
- Atlantis was the true antediluvian world.
- The oldest colony founded by the Atlanteans was in Egypt.
- The Atlanteans were the first people to use iron and bronze.
- The Atlanteans invented the first alphabet.
- Atlantis was destroyed by a natural disaster, such as an earthquake or volcanic eruption.
- A few people escaped on rafts and ships.

# A lack of evidence

Donnelly based his theories on Plato's account of Atlantis and his own study of a variety of sciences, including **zoology** and **geology**. In the 19th century, these "new sciences" were only beginning to be studied and taken seriously. Donnelly's claims captured the imaginations of a great many people. However, more traditional scientists dismissed them as nonsense. They wanted to see hard evidence and Donnelly could not produce any.

## Sun worship

*From his study of ancient religions, Donnelly concluded that the people of Atlantis worshiped the sun. He believed their religion spread to Ancient Egypt and Peru. Since then, **archaeologists** have discovered many Egyptian paintings showing worship of the sun god, Ra, and mysterious carvings of the sun in the Nazca desert in Peru. Could Donnelly's theories be true?*

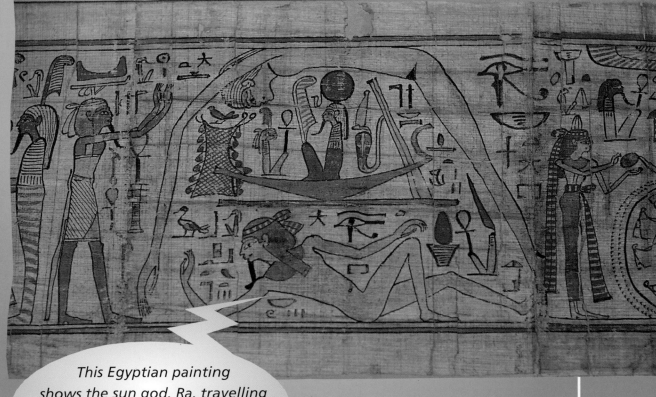

*This Egyptian painting shows the sun god, Ra, travelling in his solar barge between Nut, the sky goddess (above), and Geb, the earth god (below).*

# Other Theories

Donnelly's book sparked huge interest in Atlantis. Thousands of books, articles, and short stories followed. The name of Atlantis was used on everything from ships to a region of the planet Mars. Despite its popularity, many people dismissed Donnelly's claims. Even so, hundreds of other theories grew from it. Some are based in science. Others are completely made up. Here are just some of them:

This huge crater in Arizona was formed when a giant meteorite hit the earth about 50,000 years ago. Could an even larger meteorite have hit Atlantis?

## Bombardment from space

Several theories suggest that Atlantis was destroyed when an enormous **meteorite** hit the earth. In 1976 German scientist and engineer Otto Muck published his book *The Secret of Atlantis*. He discusses two huge depressions on the floor of the western Atlantic Ocean. He states that it is likely that these four-mile (seven-kilometer) deep dents are **impact craters**. Scientifically, it is possible. In 1920, a meteorite weighing 65 tons struck Namibia, Africa. It is the largest meteorite yet known. According to Muck, the Atlantic meteorite was 6 miles (10 kilometers) wide. He claims that it also split the Atlantic Ocean open along the Mid-Atlantic Ridge. This ridge is a long chain of underwater mountains that run down the middle of the Atlantic Ocean. Science has since proven this to be untrue.

12

# Evidence from eels

In his book, Muck also suggested that the sinking of Atlantis could explain the mysterious **migrations** of eels. Each year, European eels leave their river homes. They swim from the Atlantic Ocean to the Sargasso Sea to breed. Then the tiny **elvers** begin an incredible 3,600-mile (6,000-kilometer), three-year-long journey home. They are carried on the warm waters of the Gulf Stream current. Muck wondered why the eels should risk such a long and dangerous journey. He suggested that the Gulf Stream once circled Atlantis. Thus, the eels were carried to fresh water by a much shorter, more direct route. When Atlantis sank, it broke the flow of the Gulf Stream and made the eels' journey much longer.

## Pyramid parallels

*Some people have tried to link Atlantis to the **civilizations** of Central and South America. Lewis Spence, a writer from Scotland, wrote several books on the subject from the 1920s through the 1940s. For example, he pointed to similarities between the pyramids built by the Mayans in Mexico and those built by the ancient Egyptians, whose country was supposedly ruled by Atlantis. But many historians do not believe that the two are linked. They believe these events occurred independently in each place.*

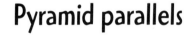

*Because they are similar in shape to the pyramids of Ancient Egypt, Spence suggested that the designs of the Mayan pyramids in Mexico were influenced by Atlantean culture.*

# Atlantis Found?

If Atlantis did exist, where was it located? According to Plato, it was "an island situated in front of the **straits** which you call the Pillars of Hercules." This places Atlantis to the west of the Straits of Gibraltar—called the Pillars of Hercules by the Greeks—in the Atlantic Ocean. But not everyone agrees. People have suggested that Atlantis was in South America, North America, Scandinavia, the Canary Islands, and Greenland. On the following pages, you will read about the various places Atlantis might have been.

## Lost in the jungle

The English explorer Percy Fawcett was convinced that Atlantis was in Brazil. There, **archaeologists** were already beginning to discover the ancient ruins of long-lost cities in the jungle. His belief was based on a stone statue he had been given. He was sure it came from Atlantis. In 1924, Fawcett set off to find Atlantis. He was never seen again. Rumors say he was killed by a local chief, or he had found his lost city and loved it so much that he chose to live out his life there.

*The summit of the Rock of Gibraltar. In ancient times, this rock and Jebel Musa, in modern Morocco, were known as the "Pillars of Hercules." They mark the border between the Mediterranean Sea and the Atlantic Ocean.*

## St. Brendan's Isle

*In the Middle Ages, many people believed in the existence of mysterious islands in the Atlantic Ocean. These were called "paradise islands." They were thought to be perfect worlds. The islands were marked on medieval maps. Many went on voyages to find them. St. Brendan's Isle was discovered by St. Brendan, an Irish monk, in the 6th century A.D. Some people believe there is a connection between these islands and Atlantis.*

## Northern Europe

In his 1976 book *Atlantis of the North*, German scholar Dr. Jürgen Spanuth tried to prove that Atlantis was located off the northwest coast of Germany. He thought it was among a group of sunken islands. He also claimed that the people of Atlantis were the early ancestors of the Vikings. No evidence has yet been found to support his theories.

## Antarctic Atlantis

*Gods of the New Millennium* was published in 1996 by American author Alan F. Alford. Alford suggests that Atlantis may have been in Antarctica. He draws his conclusion from Plato's accounts. Plato says that Atlantis existed about 12,000 years ago. Alford says that at that time Antarctica was ice-free and has only been frozen for about 6,000 years. According to Alford, Antarctica was inhabited by the Atlanteans. He believes they went from Antarctica to other parts of the world, including Egypt, where they built the pyramids. It is true that Antarctica was not always a frozen continent. However, geological studies of ancient rock and ice samples show that Antarctica was largely covered in ice two to three million years ago. These facts disprove Alford's theory.

# Earth Movements

In his book, Ignatius Donnelly suggested that the likeliest site for Atlantis was the Azores. The Azores are a group of islands in the middle of the North Atlantic Ocean. His theory has now been disproved by geologists.

## The earth's crust

The earth's hard, outer crust is not one single layer of rock. It is split into seven huge pieces and numerous smaller ones. These pieces are called plates. The plates are constantly floating or drifting on the layer of red-hot, liquid rock called magma. This movement is called **continental** drift. Ordinarily, we cannot feel the earth's crust moving. However, when the plates collide or pull apart violently, we experience earthquakes and volcanoes.

*This is an island in the Azores, which Donnelly believed to be Atlantis. Since then, his theory has been proved to be scientifically impossible.*

## Mid-Atlantic Ridge

In the middle of the Atlantic Ocean, two plates of the earth's crust are slowly pulling apart. Over millions of years, magma has welled up to fill the gap, hardened, and pushed up again. This process is called sea-floor spreading. It formed a chain of mountains that runs the entire length of the Atlantic Ocean. The Mid-Atlantic Ridge is the longest mountain range on Earth. It splits the Atlantic Ocean in two. In a few places, the ridge rises to the surface. The Azores are one of those places.

# Disproving Donnelly

Donnelly believed that the Azores were the mountain tops of the sunken island Atlantis. In 1882, when Donnelly's book came out, the Mid-Atlantic Ridge had been discovered. However, very little was known about its **geology**. The modern science of oceanography, the study of the oceans, has shown that the Azores are, in fact, islands. They formed as a result of the seafloor spreading. The Azores grew up from the ocean floor, not sink into it. They cannot be Atlantis.

## Continental drift

*In 1915, a German scientist, Alfred Wegener, was the first to suggest that plates making up the earth's crust move. He proposed that about 200 million years ago, all the land masses were joined together. According to Wegener, it was one huge continent, Pangaea. It was surrounded by a huge ocean, Panthalassa. Over millions of years, the plates drifted apart. As Pangaea split, the continents and oceans we have today were formed. Wegener's theory was not taken seriously until the 1960s. Then geologists discovered that the plates did indeed move. They also found fossil evidence of plants and dinosaurs to support the idea of a single continent, as Wegener said.*

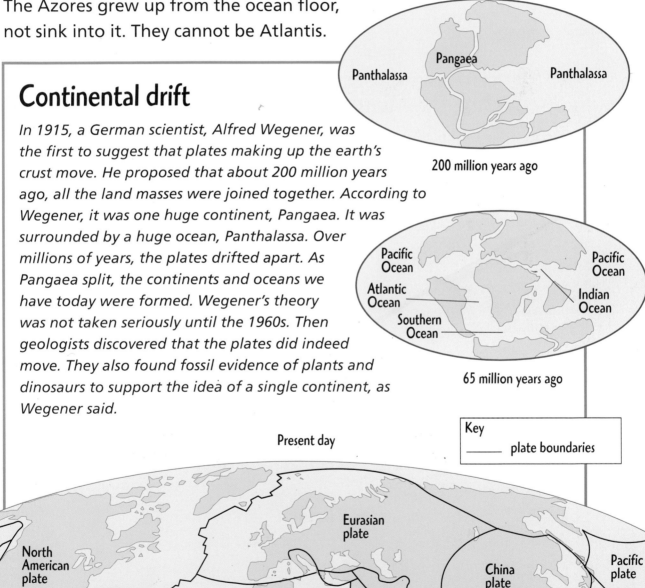

200 million years ago

65 million years ago

Present day

Key
—— plate boundaries

# Looking at the Past

Could Atlantis have been on the Greek island of Crete, in the Mediterranean Sea? One of the strongest theories about its location points to this possibility. It was there, about 4,000 years ago, that a mighty **civilization** grew up. It shared many similarities with Plato's island of Atlantis. Could they be one and the same? Some scientists think they might be.

*Part of the ruined Minoan palace of Knossos. Some scientists believe that the Atlanteans and Minoans may have been one and the same.*

## Rediscovering the Minoans

*Our knowledge of the Minoans, the people who lived on Crete about 4,000 years ago, comes from archaeological evidence. In 1900, British **archaeologist** Sir Arthur Evans began excavating the magnificent royal palace at Knossos. He uncovered a civilization far more advanced and sophisticated than anything yet found in Europe. Evans called it Minoan after a **legendary** ruler, King Minos.*

## Similarities

From Evans' discoveries, other scholars recognized similarities between Minoan and Atlantean cultures. The Minoans built their towns around magnificent palaces. The largest and grandest was at Knossos. Did Plato hear about this? Is the description of the royal palace in Atlantis based on it? Had the story reached the ancient Egyptians, who had passed it to Solon as Plato claimed?

Evans also found many paintings and sculptures of bulls. Bulls were sacred animals for the Minoans. Plato described a similar **cult** of bull-worship on Atlantis.

Finally, both the Minoans and Atlanteans met a mysterious and violent end. In about 1500 B.C., Minoan civilization was destroyed. It was struck by natural disasters, including earthquakes and tidal waves. Plato describes Atlantis as being destroyed by "violent earthquakes and floods."

*A **fresco** from Knossos showing the ancient sport of bull-leaping. Both the Atlanteans and Minoans were said to have worshiped bulls.*

## ... and differences

So could Crete be Atlantis? Despite the similarities, there are differences that need to be examined. Crete was not a round island. Plato describes Atlantis as round. Crete did not sink into the sea and vanish without trace. Atlantis supposedly did. Crete is not located in the Atlantic Ocean. However, clay tablets and discs from Crete may hold the answers. Archaeologists have yet to decode the Minoan script, Linear A, in which they were written. What secrets will be uncovered when the message is decoded?

# A Violent Volcano

Many experts have linked the collapse of Minoan **civilization** to the violent eruption of Thera. Thera was a volcanic island about 66 miles (110 kilometers) north of Crete. Or could Thera itself have been Atlantis?

*Excavations at Akrotiri on Santorini, or Thera, have uncovered a great city in Minoan style. Could these be the long-lost ruins of Atlantis?*

## Thera erupts

The traditional date given for the eruption of Thera is 1450 B.C. This is about the same time as the Minoan collapse. The explosion was so violent that most of Thera was blown away. Only a small crescent shaped island, Santorini, remains. The eruption may have caused tidal waves, flooding, and earth tremors on Crete. Recent **archaeological** evidence suggests, however, that Thera may have erupted about 200 years earlier. Therefore, it may not have destroyed Minoan Crete. Even if these two dates matched, it still puts the destruction of Atlantis 900 years before Solon, not 9,000 as in Plato's account.

# Thera as Atlantis

Was Thera the **catastrophe** that destroyed Atlantis? Greek archaeologist Professor Spyridon Marinatos thought so. He also believed that Thera was linked to Crete because the Minoan culture had spread throughout the Mediterranean. In 1967, he began excavating at Akrotiri, in the southwest of Santorini. Buried under layers of volcanic ash, Marinatos found the remains of a great city. He uncovered streets of Minoan-style houses and **frescoes**. This proved that a highly advanced civilization once lived there. He thought that the scribe who recorded the events had simply written the wrong dates down. He assumed the scribe multiplied 900 by 10. If that is true, it explains why Plato says that Atlantis existed 9,000 years before Solon.

Was Thera itself Atlantis? Scientists know that the eruption destroyed the island. The central part of the island sank into the sea. Could this explain the mystery?

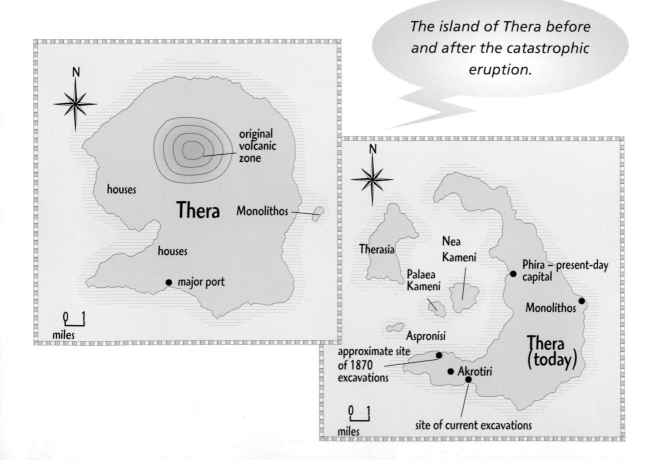

The island of Thera before and after the catastrophic eruption.

# Other Sunken Cities

Atlantis hunters have not given up hope of finding the lost land. They point to the many examples of ancient places that were found thousands of years after sinking. These include the ancient Greek port of Apollonia in Libya, built around 630 B.C., and Port Royal, the pirate city described below. One day, the ruins of Atlantis may be added to the list.

## Lost kingdom

A group of rocks called the "Seven Sisters" lies six miles (10 kilometers) off Land's End, the southernmost tip of Britain. According to **legend,** these rocks mark the site of a kingdom that once linked Britain to France. The kingdom was called Lyonesse. In the 5th century A.D., Lyonesse was swallowed by a huge wave and disappeared beneath the sea. There was only one survivor. Since then, local fishers have caught pieces of buildings and other remains in their nets. They claim that these come from Lyonesse.

One of the "Seven Sisters" rocks off Land's End, England. This was said to be where the lost kingdom of Lyonesse sank into the sea.

## Diving dilemmas

*There are many problems with diving to look for ruins. As divers go deeper, the weight of the water pressing down on them increases. This produces bubbles of gas in their blood. If they surface too quickly, the bubbles cause a painful, sometimes deadly, condition called the "bends." To avoid this, divers spend time in a decompression chamber. There, they slowly and safely return to normal pressure.*

## Port Royal

On June 7, 1692, the pirate harbor of Port Royal, Jamaica, sank into the sea. Just before midday, the city was hit by a massive and disastrous earthquake. The whole waterfront, including streets, houses, and shops, slid into the sea. A huge tidal wave swept over the city. In two short minutes, two-thirds of the city was swallowed up. Two thousand people were dead. For hundreds of years, the ruins of Port Royal lay underwater. Then, in 1959, an American ship, *Sea Diver*, explored the site. The ship was equipped with **echo sounders** and **radar**. In the 1960s, divers and **archaeologists** continued to search the ruins. Thousands of **artifacts** were found.

# Strange Stories

There are many different theories about Atlantis. Some have been very carefully tested using science and history. Science has disproved many theories. Because the question has yet to be answered, new theories are being put forward all the time. Some theories are not based on science. Some theories on Atlantis are put forward by **occultists**. They approach the search for Atlantis using the supernatural.

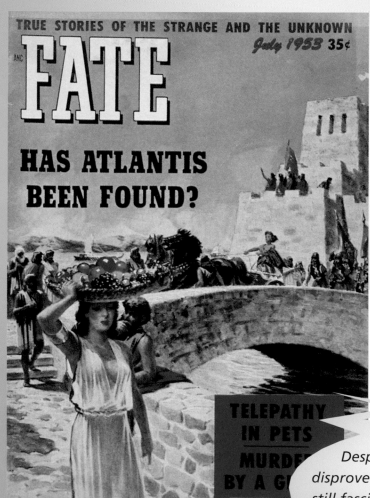

## Atlantis rising

*Atlantology is the name given to the study, scientific or otherwise, of Atlantis. Many Atlantologists believe that one day, Atlantis will rise again. This does not mean that the island will physically rise from the sea. Rather, people will embrace the qualities and virtues of goodness, courage, and wisdom that made Atlantis great. Atlantis can be reborn in ideas and hopes.*

*Despite many theories having been disproved, the possibility of finding Atlantis still fascinates **archaeologists** and occultists.*

# The fourth race

In 1877 Russian occultist Helena Blavatsky published a huge book called *Isis Unveiled*. It contained one page on Atlantis. In *Isis Unveiled*, Blavatsky presented her theory about the mystery of Atlantis. She claimed that the people of Atlantis were the fourth "race" on Earth. She said they were a super-human people who lived long before human beings. She believed Atlanteans had amazing **psychic** powers. However, they were corrupted by a great dragon king, Thevetat, and turned into wicked magicians. The magicians started a war that destroyed Atlantis.

In her next book, *The Secret Doctrine*, published after she died, Madame Blavatsky tells more about Atlantis. In the book she comments on an ancient text. The text is said to have been written in Atlantis. She tells how the survivors of Atlantis settled in Egypt and built the pyramids about 100 thousand years ago. But modern science shows that the earliest pyramids were actually built around 2600 B.C.

A huge stone statue of a Toltec warrior.

## Toltec ancestors

In the 1890s, another occultist, W. Scott-Elliott, claimed to be able to read the Akashic Records. These records are said to hold the history of ancient wisdom. They exist outside of ordinary time. He claimed that the records told him that Atlantis existed one million years ago. The records state that there were seven races of Atlanteans. One of these was the Toltecs. Historically, the Toltecs lived in Mexico. They built their capital at Tula, north of Mexico City, around A.D. 900.

# A False Start

In the 1920s, an American **clairvoyant**, Edgar Cayce, claimed that he had lived one of his past lives in Atlantis. According to Cayce, Atlantis had a rocky history. He said Atlantis stretched from the Sargasso Sea to the Azores. It was about the size of Europe, and the land and **civilization** had been destroyed twice. This caused the mainland to split into islands. The last of Atlantis disappeared near the Bahamas. In 1940, Cayce predicted that this part of Atlantis would rise again, around 1968. Would his prediction come true?

## Fakes and frauds

*In the 1870s, German **archaeologist** Heinrich Schliemann discovered the ruins of the ancient city of Troy, in Turkey. This is the site of the legendary Trojan War. Forty years later, his grandson Paul claimed that Troy and Atlantis had been allies. He said that his grandfather found a bowl at Troy. Inscribed on the bowl were the words "From King Cronos of Atlantis." Archaeologists later proved that the bowl was a fake.*

## The Bimini Road

Early in 1968, an archaeologist, Dr. J. Manson Valentine, found a J-shaped pathway. It was made of rectangular stone slabs. It covered about 2,300 feet (700 meters). The path was several feet underwater. It lay off the coast of North Bimini, Bahamas. The path became known as the Bimini Road. Had Atlantis been found, as Cayce had predicted? One Atlantis hunter had no doubt. He claimed that the stones were part of an ancient Atlantean temple. One of them might even be the head of a stone statue.

Scientists disagreed. Some said that the pavement was a natural formation. Others thought it could be man-made, but that it was likely to be the remains of a sunken sea wall. In 1981, during an oceanographic survey of the area, the US **Geological** Survey shed some light on the subject. They found that the "road" had formed naturally. They also found out that the path was between 2500 and 3500 years old. It is too young to be Atlantis.

An intriguing glimpse of the Bimini Road. You can just pick out the J-shaped pathway of stones beneath the water.

# In Conclusion

Can science solve the mystery of Atlantis? It seems unlikely. So far, there is no proof that Atlantis was a real place. Plato's accounts are the only source we have for its existence. The story they tell was already 9,000 years old when Plato wrote it. We know that ancient Egyptians and Solon are historical facts. But there is much we can't prove. Is all the information in Plato's writings factual? How could we tell? Today, experts generally agree that Plato was describing his own city, Athens. Once, Athens had been rich and powerful, as Atlantis had been. Was Plato sending a warning to his community? Perhaps he saw the Athenians becoming corrupt and greedy. This is how he described the Atlanteans. Was he trying to save Athenians from destroying themselves?

*The city of Athens, Greece, today. Was Plato really talking about Athens, not Atlantis, in his accounts? If so, what was he trying to teach the Athenians?*

# Could Crete be Atlantis?

If Atlantis did exist, the most likely location seems to be the island of Crete in the Mediterranean Sea. **Archaeologists** have uncovered many similarities between Minoan culture and that of Plato's Atlantis. Scientific findings prove that Crete was struck by earthquakes and floods. These may have been caused by the violent eruption of nearby Thera. The search for answers seems to lead to more questions.

## Fact or fiction?

*In 1975, a special conference was held at the University of Indiana to debate the question, "Atlantis, fact or fiction?" The experts who argued that Atlantis is a myth presented the winning argument. It is true that there is no solid proof. But, there is no solid proof that it doesn't exist!*

## What do you think?

You have read about Atlantis and the theories for and against its existence. Can you draw any conclusions? Do any of the theories seem to answer the question for you? Do you have any theories of your own? Do you think we are close to solving the mystery of Atlantis?

Review the information presented. Think about the mysterious Bimini Road. What were the natural forces that laid it? Were the Atlanteans really the Minoans? Try to keep an open mind. If scientists throughout history didn't investigate the strange or mysterious, many discoveries would be lost. Remember, having no proof is very different from proving something wrong.

# Glossary

**antediluvian** time before the great flood described in the Bible

**archaeologist** scientist who studies the past by looking at ancient ruins and remains

**artifact** ancient object, such as a pot, a piece of jewelery, or a weapon

**catastrophe** sudden, widespread disaster

**civilization** group of people and the society in which they live

**clairvoyant** person who claims to have the power to look into the future or see objects out of sight

**continent** large area of land

**cult** religious group or a great liking or interest in something

**echo sounder** device used to measure the depth of water and to map the features of the sea bed, using pulses of sound that hit parts of the seafloor and return as echoes

**elver** young eel

**empire** all the lands controlled by one country or a powerful leader

**fresco** painting done on wet plaster

**geology** science that studies the history of the earth

**impact crater** deep hole in the ground left when a meteorite hits the earth

**legendary** based on a legend, which may or may not be true

**meteorite** space rock that originally comes from comets and sometimes crashes into the earth

**migration** long journey made by some fish, birds, and mammals between their feeding and breeding grounds

**occultist** person who is interested in the supernatural

**philosopher** person who studies the meaning of life and the universe

**pinnacle** decorative turret on a building's roof

**privileged** lucky or honored

**psychic** person who claims to be able to read people's minds and to see into the future

**radar** device used to locate objects and determine their size and the speed at which they are moving

**strait** narrow channel connecting two large areas of water

**subdue** to calm

**zoology** scientific study of animals

# More Books to Read

Barber, Nicola. *The Search for Lost Cities.* Austin, Tex.: Raintree Steck-Vaughn, 1998.

Innes, Brian. *Where Was Atlantis?* Austin, Tex.: Raintree Steck-Vaughn, 1999.

Millard, Anne. *Lost Civilizations.* Brookfield, Conn.: Millbrook Press, 1996.

Stefoff, Rebecca. *Finding the Lost Cities.* New York: Oxford University Press, 1997.

# Index

Alford, Alan F.  15

Antarctica  15

Apollonia  22

archaeology  4, 11, 14–15, 18–21, 23, 24, 26

Athens  6, 9, 28

Atlantis
   civilization  4, 8–10,18–19
   destruction of  7, 9, 10, 19, 26
   films about  5
   location of  7, 10, 13–16, 26

Azores  10, 16–17, 26

Bahamas  26

Bimini Road  26–27, 29

Blavatsky, Madame Helena  25

Brazil  14

bull worship  19

Cayce, Edgar  26

Crete  18–20, 29

diving  23

Donnelly, Ignatius  10–12, 16–17

Earth's crust  16–17

eels  13

Egypt  6–7, 10–11, 13, 15, 25, 28

Evans, Sir Arthur  18

Fawcett, Percy  14

geology  11, 15–17

Greece  4, 6–7, 28

Libya  7

Lyonesse  22

Marinatos, Professor Spyridon  21

meteorite  12

Mexico  13, 25

Mid-Atlantic Ridge  12, 16-17

Muck, Otto  12–13

occultists  24–25

oceanography  17, 27

Peru  11

Pillars of Hercules  7, 14

Plato  4, 6, 8–11, 14-15, 18-19, 20-21, 28–29

Port Royal  23

Poseidon  8–9

pyramids  13, 15

St. Brendan's Isle  15

Socrates  6

Solon  6–7, 9, 18, 20-21, 28

Spanuth, Dr. Jürgen  15

Spence, Lewis  13

sun worship  11

Thera  20–21, 29

Toltecs  25

Troy  26

Wegener, Alfred  17

Zeus  9

zoology  11